GĪTĀMṚTAM

GĪTĀMṚTAM

The Essential Teachings of the Bhagavadgītā

Anantanand Rambachan

MOTILAL BANARSIDASS PUBLISHERS
PRIVATE LIMITED ● DELHI

First Edition: Delhi, 1993

ISBN : 81-208-1167-4

Also available at:

MOTILAL BANARSIDASS

41 U.A. Bungalow Road, Jawahar Nagar, Delhi 110 007
120 Royapettah High Road, Mylapore, Madras 600 004
16 St. Mark's Road, Bangalore 560 001
Ashok Rajpath, Patna 800 004
Chowk, Varanasi 221 001

PRINTED IN INDIA

BY JAINENDRA PRAKASH JAIN AT SHRI JAINENDRA PRESS,
A-45 NARAINA, PHASE I, NEW DELHI 110 028
AND PUBLISHED BY NARENDRA PRAKASH JAIN FOR
MOTILAL BANARSIDASS PUBLISHERS PVT. LTD.,
BUNGALOW ROAD, DELHI 110 007

for Surujrattan

Contents

Preface

This book is an amended version of a series of introductory public lectures on the *Bhagavadgītā* which were delivered in Trinidad (October, 1992). These lectures were sponsored by the National Council for Indian Culture, and I am grateful to the Council for inviting me to deliver these.

I am thankful to Dr. Jon Moline, Dean of St. Olaf College, for a small grant to support the preparation of this manuscript. Mark Christianson assisted with the typing and formatting and Inga Velde offered many valuable editorial suggestions.

I want to acknowledge my gratitude to Craig Rice of the Academic Computing Center of St. Olaf College who generously and readily gave of his time and expertise to make the publication of this book possible.

Chapter 1

"I Manifest from Age to Age" (4:8)

The *Bhagavadgītā* (Song of God) derives its name from the fact of being a dialogue between Kṛṣṇa, referred to as *bhagavān*, and his friend and disciple, Arjuna. Why is the title *bhagavān* used in reference to Kṛṣṇa? The *Viṣṇu Purāṇa* defines *bhagavān* and, by implication, the person to whom the word should be applied:

> *utpattiṁ pralayaṁ caiva bhūtānāmāgatiṁ gatim*
> *vetti vidyāmavidyāṁ ca sa vācyo bhagavāniti*
>
> The One is called *bhagavān* who knows the beginning and end of all things, the birth and death of all beings, and the difference between knowledge and ignorance (6.5.78).

On the basis of this definition, it is obvious that the title can only be properly applied to God. It is used as a prefix for Kṛṣṇa since he is regarded as an *avatāra*, that is, an incarnation of God. The term *avatāra* is derived from the root *avatṛ* (to descend), and indicates, therefore, the embodiment of divinity in the world.

At several points in chapters 2 and 3 of the *Bhagavadgītā*, Kṛṣṇa's remarks to Arjuna clearly point to his identity as an incarnation. At the beginning of chapter 3, for example, he explains that he had, in earlier times, taught the paths of wisdom and action to different spiritual aspirants. Later on in the same chapter, he uses himself as an example of the liberated person who has nothing personally to gain from action, but who continues to engage in work for the welfare of all beings. "If I should cease to work," says Kṛṣṇa, "these worlds would fall into ruin and I should be the creator of disordered life and destroy these people" (3:22–24).

Arjuna, however, does not follow up on any of these suggestions by inquiring about Kṛṣṇa's nature. Kṛṣṇa then begins chapter 4 by tracing the succession of disciples through which the wisdom of the *Bhagavadgītā* was transmitted.

> I taught this imperishable *yoga* to Vivasvān; Vivasvān taught it to Manu, and Manu imparted it to Ikṣvāku. Thus handed down from one to another, the royal sages knew it until that *yoga* was lost to the world with the long passage of time (4:1–2).

The same wisdom is being imparted to Arjuna, explains Kṛṣṇa, because of Arjuna's status as Kṛṣṇa's devotee and friend.

Arjuna immediately detects what he considers to be a contradiction in Kṛṣṇa's statement, and voices his bewilderment. Vivasvān's birth, Arjuna knows, was much earlier than Kṛṣṇa's. How can Kṛṣṇa claim to be the teacher of Vivasvān at the beginning of the creation? It is this inquiry of Arjuna which elicits from Kṛṣṇa the most explicit discussion of his nature as the incarnation. In two of the most important and often-quoted verses of the *Bhagavadgītā*, he explains the purpose of his divine descent.

> *yadā yadā hi dharmasya glānir bhavati bhārata*
> *abhyutthānam adharmasya tadā'tmānaṁ sṛjāmy aham*
>
> Whenever there is a decline of righteousness and a rise of unrighteousness, then I manifest myself, O Bhārata [Arjuna].
>
> *paritrāṇāya sādhūnāṁ vināśāya ca duṣkṛtām*
> *dharmasaṁsthāpanārthāya saṁbhavāmi yuge yuge*
>
> For the protection of the virtuous, for the destruction of the evildoers, and for the establishment of righteousness, I manifest from age to age (4:7–8).

These two verses offer a comprehensive statement about the circumstances and purpose of the *avatāra*. We ought, therefore, to look at Kṛṣṇa's words carefully.

We must first note the use of the term *dharma*. Derived from the root *dhṛ* (to sustain or support), it refers in this context to the network of values and actions that preserves the harmony and well-being of the cosmos. The opposite of *dharma* is *adharma*, that which brings about the disintegration of order in the universe. It is the loss of wisdom and the consequent collapse of those values necessary for the welfare of creation which instigates the descent of the divine. Scriptural accounts of this descent usually begin with graphic descriptions of chaos and oppression.

If the incarnation is necessitated by a breakdown of *dharma*, it is important to note that Kṛṣṇa does not indicate any limit to the number of occasions and times that God may choose to manifest Godself. This is indicated by the repetition of the word *yadā* (whenever). As an illustration of divine freedom, God alone chooses the occasions and frequency of God's manifestations. God determines the point at which the decline of *dharma* necessitates God's direct intervention.

What are the activities in which the *avatāra* engages? Three areas or kinds of actions are specified here:

1. *paritrāṇāya sādhūnāṁ* (the protection of the good). It is important to note that although Kṛṣṇa mentions in 4:7 that he incarnates when there is a decline of *dharma* and a rise of *adharma*, he does not speak in 4:8 about the protection of *dharma*. He speaks instead of the protection of virtuous or righteous persons. The reason is that righteousness is only meaningfully and effectively secured by protecting those who abide by its dictates. Its protection is assured by guaranteeing the freedom to exercise its principles in a community. Justice is not protected by its preservation in the law codes and manuals of an unjust society.

2. *vināśāya ca duṣkṛtām* (the destruction of the wicked). If *dharma* is secured by protecting those who live according to its dictates, *adharma* is destroyed by the restraint, reform and, in some cases, the death of those who are its proponents. The gentle methods of argument and persuasion, however, are always employed before the *avatāra* applies the last option. For persons like Rāvaṇa and Kaṁsa, physical death at the hands of the incarnation provides a new opportunity for moral and spiritual growth.

3. *dharmasaṁsthāpanārthāya* (the establishment of righteousness). In addition to protecting the virtuous and punishing the wicked, the *avatāra* engages in a variety of activities for the establishment of *dharma*. These may include teaching, as in the *Bhagavadgītā*, and providing examples of righteous action.

It is not necessary for any particular incarnation to accomplish the above three purposes. A divine descent may be limited to the fulfillment of one or two of these aims.

The Hindu teaching about the *avatāra* emphasizes the belief in a God who cares about the world and those who dwell in it. God cares enough to enter the world to restore righteousness when we create disharmony and chaos. This teaching is also a belief that the values of love, truth, and justice will always triumph. We have God's assurance that *adharma* will never ultimately prevail. "God," as S. Radhakrishnan puts it, "does not stand aside when we abuse our freedom and cause disequilibrium. He does not simply wind up the world, set it on the right track, and then let it jog along by itself. His loving hand is steering it all the time."[1]

The manifestation of the *avatāra* differs from the birth of a *jīva* (human being) by the fact that it is not the consequence of past *karma* (actions). The human being is born because of the necessity to experience the effects of actions performed in previous embodiments. Birth is an effect and its causes may be traced back to actions performed in earlier existences. The descent of the *avatāra*, however, is not a necessity conditioned by any earlier actions performed by God. It is an expression of God's eternal freedom and compassion.

It is clear, however, that even God does not manifest Godself into the world without a desire. A "desireless action" is a contradiction in terms, since all actions, including those of God, are prompted by some kind of desire. We may choose the kinds of desires which motivate our actions, but as long as we live and act in the world, our actions will be initiated by desires. In the case of God, however, these desires are not for the fulfillment of any selfish purpose born out of a sense of limitation. The *avatāra*, as we have just noted, is motivated by a desire to protect the good, to destroy evil, and to establish justice and righteousness.

Unlike the ordinary human being, the *avatāra* is never a victim of self-ignorance (*avidyā*). This is a fact reiterated by Kṛṣṇa in the *Bhagavadgītā*.

> Though I am unborn and imperishable and Lord of all beings, yet ruling over my own nature (*prakṛti*), I am born by my own power (*māyā*) (4:6).

God's power of creation is referred to here as *māyā*. Through *māyā* the entire universe and all living things come into being. God is the controller of *māyā*, the master of creation, while we become its victims. Although (as we shall see in greater detail later) we are the *ātman* (Self) which is never subject to birth or death and which is beyond all change (2:20–24), we erroneously take ourselves to be identical with the physical body and claim all of its characteristics as integral to ourselves. The *avatāra*, however, is never deceived about the truth of himself as the unborn and imperishable Lord of all creation. He uses the material body as an instrument without ever becoming identified with it, fully conscious of his divine status and glory.

God's control of his creative power is obvious in the fact that, unlike the human being, God can manifest wherever, whenever, and in whatever form he chooses. The laws of creation to which we are subject are in God's hands. He is never limited by his material embodiment.

> I know the beings of the past, present, and future, but no one knows me (7:26).

The *avatāra* should not be totally identified with the particular bodily form in which he may choose to walk among us. That form comes and goes, but the nature of the incarnation is timeless and eternal. While the *avatāra* may appear to be in the world, the truth is that the world is in the *avatāra*. He exists within and supports all things.

> This entire universe is pervaded by me in my unmanifest form; all beings find their support in me and not I in them (9:4).

In the *Kiṣkindhākāṇḍa* of Tulasıdāsa's *Rāmāyaṇa*, Śrī Rāma taught Hanumān that the true devotee is one who regards the self as the servant of God, whose form incorporates the entire universe of moving and unmoving realities.[2]

The purpose of the *avatāra*, as we have seen, is threefold: the protection of the good, the destruction of evil, and the establishment of righteousness. One of the primary ways in which *dharma* is established is through the reiteration of eternal truths. While the *Bhagavadgītā* sets out to do this, it also reinterprets these truths in the context of a new situation and challenge. The wisdom of the *Upaniṣads* is offered in an accessible form, and the achievement of the *Bhagavadgītā* is summarized beautifully in one of the verses of the *Bhagavadgītā dhyānam*:

> *sarvopaniṣado gāvo dogdhā gopālanandanaḥ*
> *pārtho vatsaḥ sudhīr bhoktā dugdhaṁ gītāmṛtaṁ mahat*

> All the *Upaniṣads* are the cows; the cowherd boy, Kṛṣṇa, is the milkman; Arjuna is the calf, while all people of pure minds are the drinkers; the milk is the immortal teaching of the *Gītā*.

Notes

1. *Bhagavadgītā*, trans., S. Radhakrishnan, p. 155.
2. See A. Rambachan, *Hanumān: The Messenger of God*, pp. 33–41.

Chapter 2

"It Is Greed ... Know This to Be the Enemy Here" (3:37)

Throughout the *Bhagavadgītā*, Kṛṣṇa emphasizes the importance of wisdom and right understanding. Some of his most powerful statements on the necessity and value of knowledge are made near the end of chapter 4.

> Even if you are the most sinful of all sinners, you shall cross over all sin by the raft of knowledge (4:36).

In 4:38, he tells us that "there is no purifier in the world like knowledge." The fruit of knowledge is the immediate gain of peace (4:39). The person without wisdom is described as moving toward destruction, having failed to attain happiness in this world or in any other world (4:40).

From many statements like these in the *Bhagavadgītā*, it is clear that Kṛṣṇa's principal concern is to impart a knowledge that is vital for our well-being and happiness. What is this wisdom and how is it conducive to our welfare?

We can begin to answer this question by looking at Kṛṣṇa's diagnosis of the causes of unhappiness and unrest in our lives. The effectiveness and appropriateness of any solution can only be appreciated properly by examining the problem which it is meant to solve. A remedy cannot be proposed without identifying the disease to which it must be applied.

In chapter 3 of the *Bhagavadgītā*, Arjuna asks a crucial question of Kṛṣṇa.

> *atha kena prayukto 'yaṁ pāpaṁ carati pūruṣaḥ*
> *anicchann api vārṣṇeya balād iva niyojitaḥ*
>
> What is it that drives one to commit sin, as if by force, against one's will? (3:36)

Kṛṣṇa's answer is simple and direct:

> *kāma eṣa krodha eṣa rajoguṇasamudbhavaḥ*
> *mahāśano mahāpāpmā viddhy enam iha vairiṇam*
>
> It is greed, it is anger, born of passion; all consuming and sinful, know this as the enemy here (3:37).

In different ways, throughout the text, Kṛṣṇa identifies *kāma* (greed) as the principal cause of human unhappiness and dissatisfaction. In 16:21, for example, he says "triple is the gate of hell, destructive of the Self — greed (*kāma*), anger, and lust; therefore, these three one must abandon." In 5:23, the happy person is described as the one who is able to resist, before death, the impulses of greed (*kāma*) and anger.

While the term *kāma* is usually translated as desire, I have chosen, for a number of reasons, to equate it with greed. First, it is clear that the *Bhagavadgītā* does not see all desires as negative and, therefore, as meant to be overcome. In 7:11, Kṛṣṇa identifies himself with desires which are not opposed to *dharma* (*dharmāviruddho bhūteṣu kāmo 'smi bharatarṣabha*). If *dharma* (as discussed earlier) refers to the network of values and actions that sustains the harmony of existence, it is obvious from Kṛṣṇa's statement that those desires which do not conflict with this purpose are legitimate.

Second, we have also seen that the incarnation is possible only because of a desire for the protection of the virtuous, the destruction of evil and the restoration of righteousness.

Third, the *Bhagavadgītā* presents the ideal of performing actions for the welfare of all beings (*lokasaṅgraham*) and this ideal is certainly an approved motive.

If *kāma* does not include all desires, it must certainly refer to desires in conflict with *dharma*, desires which result in pain and suffering to others. *Kāma* also includes self-centered desires which make one forgetful of the interests and needs of others and which blind one to all but one's own gratification.

More than any particular desire, however, *kāma* refers to that generalized and unspecific state of desiring and wanting that we experience despite the fulfillment of any number of specific desires. It is a state of dissatisfaction with ourselves which no worldly gain or achievement seems to overcome or resolve. Experiencing this desire, we hope that a certain material gain or pleasurable sense experience will result in a permanent state of well-being and freedom from wanting. We then exert ourselves to achieve the object or experience of our desire. In the realization of our desire, we experience a sense of fullness and happiness. This wholeness, however, is short-lived, and soon we find ourselves again in a condition of want or *kāma*.

There are many reasons why worldly gains and pleasurable sense experiences leave us unfulfilled. The *Bhagavadgītā* repeatedly cautions us about their limitations.

> The enjoyments which are born out of contact between the senses and their respective objects are sources of unhappiness since they have a beginning and an end; a wise person does not rejoice in these (5:22).

It is obvious that no sense experience lasts forever and none, therefore, can satisfy us permanently. Material gains may be more durable than sense-pleasures, but these are also finite. In death we must, even unwillingly, give up everything.

Gains such as fame, power, and success, as attractive as they appear to be, have their own limitations. They derive their value from the fact that they are never evenly distributed. Fame, for example, would have little or no meaning if everyone enjoyed it in the same measure. As a result, the person who lusts after it usually feels threatened and insecure whenever another excels in the same arena. A person who desires to wield power may experience anxiety when another gains power and may be driven to use any means to gain and retain power to ensure that it is not shared. It is important to add, however, that the Hindu tradition does not frown upon the urge for success or wealth; nor is it naive about the necessity and significance of power. The problem arises when power and success become the principal ends of our lives. When this occurs, we can never have enough. We enter a desperate race in which there is no finishing line!

The *Bhagavadgītā* (2:62–63) gives us a detailed analysis of the sequence through which an uncontrolled desire leads to personal ruin and unhappiness.

> *dhyāyato viṣayān puṁsaḥ saṅgas teṣūpajāyate*
> *saṅgāt saṁjāyate kāmaḥ kāmāt krodho 'bhijāyate*
>
> When a person thinks of sense objects, he develops an attachment to them; from attachment comes desire and, from desire, ensues anger.
>
> *krodhād bhavati saṁmohaḥ saṁmohāt smṛtivibhramaḥ*
> *smṛtibhraṁśād buddhināśo buddhināśāt praṇaśyati*
>
> From anger comes delusion;
> from delusion follows confused memory;
> confused memory results in the loss of reason;
> from the loss of reason, one is completely ruined.

Hoping to be free from unhappiness with ourselves, we begin to *think* about a specific object. By continuously thinking about this object, we develop an *attachment* for it. The more our thoughts flow toward the object, the deeper our attachment grows. Eventually, the *attachment* gets transformed into an intense *desire* to possess the object. We then put forward various efforts to achieve the object of our desire. If these efforts are unsuccessful, for any number of reasons, the result is *anger*.

Anger deprives us of the ability for objective and impartial thinking. It blinds us to truth and reality and results in *delusion*. In anger it is very easy to jump to false conclusions and miss the most obvious facts. In such a state of delusion, there is *confusion of memory*. One forgets the relationships which one has with others and the generally accepted norms of conduct and behavior. An angry person, says Śaṅkara, may express disrespect even toward his revered teacher.

With this *confusion of memory*, one fails to *reason* properly. In memory, after all, is stored the accepted forms of proper reasoning. The loss of reason, the quality which primarily distinguishes human beings from all other life-forms, is equated with the ruin of personality and with chaos. This *Bhagavadgītā* account is an accurate description of a common sequence in the lives of many, and we can easily trace the pattern it describes in many of our own experiences.

The fulfillment of any number of desires does not lead to freedom from *kāma*. Like a raging fire, desire is never satisfied by the gain of any number of objects. Even as a fire grows stronger with the addition of fuel, desire increases with enjoyment (3:39).

In the *Rāmāyaṇa*, Rāvaṇa is portrayed as having numerous heads. Each time Rāma removes one of his heads with an arrow, a new one grows in its place. The heads of Rāvaṇa are like desires that are never eliminated through indulgence. Rāvaṇa is destroyed only when an arrow of Rāma finds his heart. Similarly, we must find a solution to the problem of want and emptiness in ourselves that goes to the heart of the problem. This is precisely what the teaching in the *Bhagavadgītā* aims to do.

Let us, however, conclude this chapter with a story that illustrates how a single desire, like a fire onto which fuel is poured, gains and multiplies.

A devotee, following the instructions of his *guru* (teacher), built a small hut some distance from a village. In this hut, he performed his prayers and practiced various spiritual disciplines. His only item of clothing was a single piece of cloth, called a *laṅgot* (loincloth). Every morning, after his bath, he would hang the wet cloth on a tree to dry. On one occasion, however, he discovered that some rats had nibbled at his cloth. He took his problem to the villagers, and the cloth was readily replaced.

A few days later the same thing happened, and the devotee returned to the villagers for a new loincloth. The villagers were quite poor themselves and explained that it was difficult for them to keep replacing the *laṅgot*. They gave him instead a cat to chase the rats away, and the immediate problem was solved.

Each morning when the devotee went to the village to collect his food for the day, he would also beg for a bowl of milk for his cat. Soon the villagers found it difficult to keep him supplied with so much milk, so they offered him a cow. The devotee had no need now to beg for milk in the village, but he required a bundle of grass from them each day for his cow.

When supplying this became difficult for the villagers, they advised him to use an uncultivated plot of land next to his hut for growing grass for his cow. The devotee took this advice and soon found it necessary to employ some labourers to help him cultivate the land and to build barns for storing all that the land produced. In a short time, he became a wealthy landlord. He was now free from his dependence on the village, but he also forgot his original purpose of practicing spiritual disciplines for growing closer to God. Each acquisition took him further away from the reason that had brought him to live outside the village.

After many years, his *guru* came to visit and went directly to the place where he knew his disciple's hut was. To his great amazement, in its place he found a huge mansion with servants everywhere. He inquired about his disciple who formerly occupied the spot. The servants led him into the house where he found his disciple dwelling in unimaginable luxury. "My child," asked the *guru*, "do you need all of this? Why did you acquire so much?" With a great sense of embarrassment, the disciple fell at the feet of his teacher and said, "You will not believe me, *guruji*, but it all came about because of a *laṅgot!*"[1]

One desire led to another until the original problem of protecting the loincloth was completely forgotten.

Notes

1. Adapted from *Tales and Parables of Sri Ramakrishna* (Madras: Sri Ramakrishna Math, 1980), pp. 18–21.

Chapter 3

"Satisfied in the Self by the Self" (2:55)

In chapter 2 we noted that the fulfillment of any particular desire — whether a desire for some material object or some sensual pleasure — does not free us permanently from craving or greed (*kāma*). We derive a limited satisfaction and continue to long for something more. Yet, unless we can be free from the craving born out of a sense of dissatisfaction with ourselves, we will never be happy.

> The person attains peace into whom all desires enter as waters enter the ocean which, filled from all sides, remains undisturbed; but not the one who clings to desires (2:70).

The ocean is always full. It remains still even though raging rivers pour their waters into it. Similarly, the mind of one who is free from *kāma* is characterized by a fullness and peace which no intruding desire can affect. This verse does suggest that, like rivers entering the ocean, desires may enter the mind of such a person. The fact that desires may not be fulfilled, however, does not cause sorrow. In contrast, one who is always plagued by desires, born out of a sense of unhappiness with oneself, never finds peace.

How can we free ourselves from craving and attain peace? In our present condition, we experience happiness only through cultivating and accomplishing various desires. If we were asked to give up our desires as a condition for being happy, such a request would seem absurd, since it is through the realization of desires that we experience happiness. In other words, without revealing a different way to personal fulfillment, it is absurd to expect that one can be free from *kāma*. The consequence of any such attempt would be frustration and a failure to gain even those limited pleasures that we derive from the fulfillment of our desires.

In chapter 2 of the *Bhagavadgītā*, Arjuna addresses a very important question to Kṛṣṇa:

> What is the description of the person who is firmly established in wisdom and steady in contemplation? How does such a person sit, walk, and talk? (2:54)

Kṛṣṇa's answer constitutes one of the best definitions of the person of wisdom in the scriptural literature of Hinduism.

> *prajahāti yadā kāmān sarvān pārtha manogatān*
> *ātmany evātmanā tuṣṭaḥ sthitaprajñas tadocyate*
>
> When all selfish desires of the mind have fallen off, and one is satisfied in the Self by the Self, then is one said to be established in wisdom (2:55).

This verse contains the essence of Kṛṣṇa's teaching in the *Bhagavadgītā*: the way to attain freedom from *kāma*. The solution is to become someone who is satisfied by the Self (*ātman*). We must assume from Kṛṣṇa's statement that the Self can fully satisfy us and grant us the peace and contentment that we fail to find elsewhere. To be satisfied by the Self (*ātmanā tuṣṭaḥ*) requires one to know the Self, for one cannot be satisfied by an unknown entity. Let us now turn, therefore, to the *Bhagavadgītā*'s teaching on the nature of the Self.

We normally think of ourselves as originating on the day that we were conceived. From birth, we move through the stages of childhood, youth, middle age, old age, and finally, death. In other words, we are born, we grow and, like all things, we die. We assume that we undergo all the changes to which our bodies are subject.

In chapter 2 of the *Bhagavadgītā*, however, Kṛṣṇa makes a remarkable statement to Arjuna. It is a claim which radically challenges the way in which we ordinarily think of ourselves.

> There was never a time when I was not, nor you, nor these rulers of men; nor will there ever be a time in the future when we shall cease to be (2:12).

If we have always existed and will always exist, it is obvious that we must be much more than our physical bodies. These, after all, have a beginning and an end. How could I be different from my body and, if I am not the same as my body, what am I?

Arjuna must have looked puzzled and bewildered by Kṛṣṇa's radical statement and so Kṛṣṇa, like an experienced teacher, uses a wonderfully suggestive example to help him understand the difference between his body and his true identity.

> *dehino 'smin yathā dehe kaumāraṁ yauvanaṁ jarā*
> *tathā dehāntaraprāptir dhīras tatra na muhyati*

> As the dweller in the body passes through childhood, youth, and old age, so also does the dweller pass into a new body; knowing this, the wise person does not grieve (2:13).

Let us reflect on this imaginative example by thinking of an old person with a good memory. Such a person can certainly recollect events and experiences that occured in childhood and youth. The old person's body, however, is not the same one of childhood and youth. The childhood body must "die" to allow the birth of a youthful body; this body, in turn, must "die" for the birth of a mature body. Yet, the old person can recollect experiences in all of these earlier bodies. Memory is possible because the person who recalls an event is the same person who has experienced the event. The memory of experiences cannot be interchanged by individuals.[1]

What does this tell us? Through the example of natural bodily changes, Kṛṣṇa draws our attention to the indweller or experiencer who remains unchanged and who witnesses and recalls all changes. If the one now dwelling in the old body were not the same one in the childhood body, recollection of early experiences would not be possible.

The childhood and youthful bodies are like different suits of clothing which the wearer uses and changes. The suits of clothing change, but the wearer is the same. In fact, Kṛṣṇa uses the example of a change of clothing to illustrate the difference between the Self (*ātman*) and the physical body.

> As a person changing worn-out clothing puts on new ones, so the dweller in the body, changing worn-out bodies, enters into others that are new (2:22).

No one takes the clothing a person wears to be identical with the wearer, even though the contemporary fashion industry would delight in such an identity. The wearer continues to be the same even when a suit of clothing is changed. Besides, one's clothing is an object of one's perception: I can see and touch it, and thus distinguish myself from it. We generally distinguish and separate ourselves from the objects of our perception.

Although we don't identify ourselves with our clothing, we naturally tend to identify ourselves with our bodies. We own all of its characteristics — like height, weight and color. Every limitation of the body is claimed by us. Since it is subject to birth, growth, change, and death, we consider ourselves to undergo all of these processes.

Is the body an object or not? It certainly is, since like other objects of perception, it can be seen and felt. Its characteristics are all known to us. In addition, we so often speak of it as "my body," indicating that we view it as an object of possession from which we are different. As an object of my knowledge, therefore, I cannot be the same as my body.

If I am not the body, perhaps I am the sense organs, the eyes or ears through which the body is known and experienced. Are the sense organs, however, known or unknown? If my eyes are blind or defective, this condition is obviously known to me. Similarly, if my hearing is imperfect, I am also aware of this fact. All of the senses, like the body, are objects of my knowledge, and I am different from them.

If I am not the body or the sense organs, am I the mind? The senses, after all, depend on the mind for their efficient functioning. A healthy ear may not register any sounds within its range unless it is backed up by an attentive mind. Similarly, we may be within the range of a speaker's voice and not hear anything if our thoughts are elsewhere. Yet, while we often identify ourselves with the thoughts and emotions of our mind, we can easily appreciate that these are objects of our awareness. Each thought occupies the mind for a limited time before passing away. I, the one who is aware of each thought, exist before the emergence of a thought, while the thought is present and after the passing of the thought. If my identity were not different from a specific thought, I would cease to be with the disappearance of that thought.

Since I am aware of my body, sense organs, and mind I must be, as the *Bhagavadgītā* teaches, different from these. By distinguishing myself from all things that are objects of my awareness, I can appreciate that my nature is pure awareness (*cit*). I am the awareness by which the body, senses, and mind are known and illumined. Awareness, in fact, reveals and illumines all objects in the universe. Awareness, however, is self-revealing and is not illumined by any other source. It is never an object like a flower or a thought since it is the Self (*ātman*), and another Self would be needed to make it an object!

> As the one sun lights up the entire world, so does the Lord of the field illumine the entire field (13:33).

If I am the *ātman*, the nature of which is pure awareness and different from the body, senses, and mind, then I can infer that the charateristics of the latter are not intrinsic to me. Unlike the body which is subject to time and change, the *ātman* is eternal and changeless. We have already seen that whereas the body changes during childhood, youth, and old age, the indweller in the body remains unchanged. Childhood, youth, and old age are like different roles played at different times by a single unchanging actor. That indweller is the *ātman*, the unchanging witness of all changes in the body and mind.

No instrument or object can bring about the destruction of the Self.

> Weapons cannot cut it; fire cannot burn it; water cannot drown it; even the wind cannot dry it.
>
> It cannot be cut, burnt, drowned, or dried. It is eternal, all-pervading, immovable, and everlasting (2:23–24).

Being eternal (*nitya*) implies existence in all periods of time. This means that for the *ātman* there is neither birth nor death.

> The *ātman* is not born, nor does it ever die. It is not subject to the process of coming into being and ceasing to be. Eternal, changeless, and ancient, it is not destroyed when the body is destroyed (2:20).

Along with definitions like eternal (*nitya*) and everlasting (*sanātana*), the *Bhagavadgītā* also describes the *ātman* to be all-pervasive (*sarvagataḥ*). An entity is said to be limited by space when it has a form, occupies space, and is not, at the same time, everywhere. By describing the *ātman* as *sarvagataḥ*, Kṛṣṇa is pointing to its limitless nature with reference to space. In fact, in the *Bhagavadgītā* (13:32) space itself is described as being all-pervading, since all things exist in space. However, space and all objects exist in and are pervaded by the *ātman*.

Ātman, like space, is everywhere one and the same. While physical bodies and thoughts differ from one person to another, awareness is the same in all beings. The awareness through which your body and thoughts are known to you is the same awareness through which I know my body and thoughts. Kṛṣṇa speaks of many bodies but one indweller.

> These bodies of the Indweller, who is eternal, indestructible, and immeasurable, are said to have an end. Therefore, fight O Bhārata (2:18).

Freedom from *kāma* is attained through the discovery of a source of fullness which does not depend on the accomplishment of desires. Kṛṣṇa teaches that this fullness can be discovered in the nature of the *ātman* (*ātmanā tuṣṭaḥ*). In our present condition, we still gain happiness primarily through the attainment of the objects of our desires.

We can appreciate, however, that happiness is not the content of any object. The same object which appears to be the source of my joy today easily becomes the cause of my unhappiness tomorrow. In addition one object can, at the same time, be the occasion for joy and sorrow in different persons. These truths help us to establish that happiness is not an object or the quality of any object. Happiness is also not to be found in any organ of the body, since one could be quite miserable with all one's bodily organs intact. Similarly, thoughts cannot be the source of happiness since they are quite capable of causing pain.

If happiness is not in any object, organ of the body, or thought, it must be, as the *Bhagavadgītā* suggests, the very nature of the *ātman*. The *ātman*, in other words, is happiness (*ānanda*).

If this is true, why do we experience happiness in the attainment of a desired object? The existence of a desire in the mind induces a restlessness for its fulfillment. When the object is gained, the agitations disappear in the satisfied condition of one's mind. In this contented mind, the happiness experienced is the nature of one's Self. The gain of the object only serves to bring about a necessary and appropriate mental condition in which this happiness is known. The appropriate state of mind can also be gained in the presence of a loved one or through listening to one's favorite music. Whatever the external or internal cause, the source of happiness is always one's own Self.

> When all selfish desires of the mind have fallen off and one is satisfied in the Self by the Self, then is one said to be established in wisdom (2:55).

Notes

1. For a detailed discussion of this verse, see *Bhagavadgītā: with the Commentary of Swami Chinmayananda*, pp. 63–65.

Chapter 4

"Work for the Welfare of the World" (3:20)

The basic human problem, as we have seen, is *kāma*, the greed born out of a sense of dissatisfaction with ourselves. Driven by this force, we develop desires of different kinds, hoping that their attainment will result in a sense of personal well-being and security. Each fulfilled desire, however, satisfies us for a limited time, and new ones are soon born to initiate the cycle all over again.

In the *Bhagavadgītā*, Kṛṣṇa teaches that we get caught in this unending web of desires because of a false understanding of ourselves. We take ourselves to be non-different from our physical bodies and claim all of their characteristics as belonging to us. While the body is born and dies, the *ātman* is unborn and eternal. The body exists in and is limited by space, but the *ātman* is all-pervasive (*sarvagataḥ*). Happiness is the very nature of the *ātman*. The fulfillment of any desire only creates the peaceful and tranquil condition in the mind which allows us to know the Self as joy. In the state of deep sleep (*suṣupti*), when the mind is free from the restlessness and agitation of desires, one also experiences happiness which is the Self. The nature of the *ātman* is eternal (*sat*) awareness (*cit*) and fullness (*ānanda*).

What are the implications and consequences of this new understanding of Self? Knowing oneself to be *saccidānanda* means, most importantly, that one ceases to be dissatisfied with oneself. One is able to accept oneself without continously desiring to be different. One becomes, in the famous words of the *Bhagavadgītā*, *ātmany evātmanā tuṣṭaḥ* (satisfied in the Self, by the Self). What a wonderful gain it is to be at peace with oneself! Such peace is a necessary condition for happiness. How can one be happy without peace (*aśāntasya kutaḥ sukham*) (2:66)?

> One whose happiness is within, who rejoices within, and whose light is within attains the eternal, having become one with the eternal (5:24).

We begin each day of our lives hoping that our various activities will result in happiness. Imagine, instead, a condition in which one no longer struggles each day to be happy, but performs each action from a state of inner fullness. Such a condition is indeed the fruit of Self-knowledge.

While a state like this may be difficult to imagine, we do, in fact, know situations when we are able to perform actions from inner fullness. Let me cite one familiar and joyful example. All of us, at one time or another, have played with a baby. When we are alone with a baby, we find it possible to accept ourselves. We are not uncomfortable or dissatisfied with ourselves because we do not feel threatened by a baby's judgment. In the company of our peers, we are likely to feel a discomfort that springs from the fear of failing to meet their expectations. In contrast, Self-acceptance in the company of a baby leads to happiness.

In a baby's company we utter the strangest of sounds and make the most unusual facial and bodily gestures. At such a time we are not struggling to be happy but expressing a happiness which the innocent love of the child invokes in us. An onlooker who has never played with a baby may find such play odd and incomprehensible, since it is outside the realm of his or her experience. Similarly, the delight of one who is *saccidānanda* and who brings a joy to all action and relationships may not be easily understood by someone who associates happiness only with the attainment of objects different from oneself.

> That which is night to all beings, in that the disciplined person keeps awake; where all beings are awake, that is night for the wise one who sees (2:69).

In this suggestive example, Kṛṣṇa's point is that the person ignorant of the nature of the *ātman* focuses the search for happiness in the objects of the world. The knower of the Self, however, is not obsessed with the acquisition of such objects, knowing that the Self is *ānanda*. The knower of Self does not look to the gain of objects for a sense of self-worth.

At this juncture, an important question arises. If one knows oneself to be the *ātman* which is *saccidānanda*, why would one want to perform any actions in the world? All actions, it may be argued, are motivated by desires which are meant for one's happiness. Now that one understands that the Self is of the nature of joy (*ānanda*), what is the motivation for acting? What purpose would inspire actions?

Kṛṣṇa is very much aware of this issue. He provides a comprehensive justification for action, showing that Self-knowledge does not eliminate or undermine one's motivation for action, but rather provides new and noble reasons to act. Let us examine the various components of his answer.

Kṛṣṇa argues that no human being has a choice between performing or not performing actions.

> *na hi kaścit kṣaṇam api jātu tiṣṭhaty akarmakṛt*
> *kāryate hy avaśaḥ karma sarvaḥ prakṛtirjair guṇaiḥ*
>
> None can remain actionless even for a moment, for everyone is helplessly driven to action by the qualities (*guṇas*) born out of nature (*prakṛti*) (3:5).

Existence in the human body, teaches Kṛṣṇa, makes action unavoidable. The body/mind complex is constituted of the *guṇas* (qualities) of *prakṛti* (nature), and these are in constant motion. If one tries to avoid action, then life itself becomes impossible. "Even the maintenance of physical life cannot be effected without action" (3:8). Self-knowledge, it must be remembered, does not imply that one no longer has any material needs, and the fulfillment of these requires the performance of action.

Certainly, one may argue, the wise person (*jñānī*) ought to have a better and higher purpose for performing actions than the mere maintenance of physical life. If the *jñānī* is driven only by the concern for maintaining life in the body, then the *jñānī* 's motivation will not be different from humans who are still subject to ignorance about themselves or even from other-than-human life forms. This is a valid argument and Kṛṣṇa certainly expects the *jñānī* to have a nobler reason for perfoming actions in the world. This reason is clearly affirmed by Kṛṣṇa in the following verse:

> *karmaṇaiva hi saṁsiddhim āsthitā janakādayaḥ*
> *lokasaṁgraham evāpi sampaśyan kartum arhasi*
>
> Janaka and others indeed achieved perfection by performing actions; with a concern for the welfare of the world, you should also perform actions (3:20).

Kṛṣṇa offers to us the example of the ancient king, Janaka, who led a life of extraordinary activity and who never found it necessary to abandon actions for the purpose of gaining Self-knowledge. Janaka also did not renounce actions after the gain of wisdom. Why did Janaka and others, even when they had nothing personal to gain from action, continue to act? In 3:20 Kṛṣṇa teaches that the welfare of the world is clearly the highest motive for action and the one by which outstanding persons, like Janaka, were inspired.

The freedom from selfish desire which knowledge of the *ātman* brings about only serves to lift action to newer and higher levels. Human motivation is not destroyed, but transformed. Kṛṣṇa's argument is that while actions are unavoidable and while actions cannot be performed without some form of desire, these desires do not have to be self-centered ones. The ideal of the *Bhagavadgītā* is dedicated and disciplined activity for the well-being of others. Self-knowledge liberates one from the narrow confines of selfish action to the freedom of serving others.

The term *lokasaṁgraham*, used by Kṛṣṇa in 3:20, is extremely inclusive. *Loka* refers not only to the world of human beings but to all existence. The compassion of the *jñānī*, in other words, has no limits.

The welfare and service of others is certainly the highest motive from which the *jñānī* can act, but Kṛṣṇa also mentions another important concern.

> *yad-yad ācarati śreṣṭhas tat-tad evetaro janaḥ*
> *sa yat pramāṇaṁ kurute lokas tad anuvaratate*
>
> Whatever a great person does is followed by others; people adopt the standards established by such a person (3:21).

It is well-known that human beings learn by example. A child imbibes its standards of conduct by imitating the behavior of its parents, and the moral tone of a society is established by its leaders and prominent citizens. It is quite significant that Kṛṣṇa refers to the importance of the *actions* of leading citizens. His point is that a leader more effectively gives direction to his or her society by the quality of actions performed and less by words spoken. When virtuous persons avoid action, society is deprived of inspiring examples of right conduct.

Kṛṣṇa's argument is a powerful incentive for good people to be involved in the leadership of their societies. If such persons are not active in society, a vacuum is created which allows those who are not motivated by *lokasaṁgraham* to become leaders and to determine the direction and values of their societies. Whatever the field of one's involvement, Kṛṣṇa implies, one's actions ought to be in harmony with one's words. When this fails to occur, a false example is set, and the ideals propounded are called into question. One's words are less likely to be misunderstood if one provides an example in action to illustrate and reinforce these words.

Kṛṣṇa gave Arjuna the example of Janaka, a person Arjuna did not know personally. Such an example may not have had a ready appeal for Arjuna, and Janaka's integration of wisdom with an active life in society may have been dismissed by Arjuna as a feat possible for persons in earlier times but not for him. In seeking to persuade an individual to adopt a particular course of action, one's appeal is always likely to be more effective if one can point to a living and familiar example. Was there anyone known to Arjuna whose actions were inspired by a concern for the well-being of others? Yes, of course. Standing right before Arjuna is his friend and teacher, Kṛṣṇa, an excellent example of the ideal of unselfish action. Kṛṣṇa reminds Arjuna of his own motive for action.

> There is nothing in the three worlds that has to be done by Me or anything unattained that has to be attained; still I engage in action.
>
> If I did not engage in work, tirelessly, people in every respect would follow my example.
>
> These worlds would perish if I did not perform action. I would be the cause of confusion of species and destroy these beings (3:22–24).

As the lord of the universe, there is nothing unaccomplished or unattained for Kṛṣṇa. All things belong to him as the creator. What motives prompt him to action? Kṛṣṇa is conscious of the impact of his example and influence on others. If he led an unproductive life of idleness, this would be the example for all those who look to him for guidance. His actions are meant for the preservation and well-being of the world. Kṛṣṇa is the ideal *karmayogī*, that is, one who cares about others and strives for their welfare even though one has nothing personal to benefit from such actions.

When we look at human behavior, we generally see the greatest commitment, dedication, and energy when actions are performed for some personal benefit. Kṛṣṇa reminds us, however, that the motive of *lokasaṁgraham* can inspire even more commitment and dedication than our own personal well- being.

> As the unlearned act from attachment to their work, so should the learned act, without attachment, desiring the welfare of the world (3:25).

The absence of a selfish motive, as we have seen, does not imply the absence of motivation. Working for others is the highest reason for involvement in the world, and this is held as the ideal for us in the *Bhagavadgītā*.

Kṛṣṇa puts such great emphasis on the performance of actions for the welfare of others that he provides us with a new and brilliant definition of the meaning of renunciation (*sannyāsa*) and the renunciant (*sannyāsin*). In the traditional understanding, the *sannyāsin* was one who renounced social and familial obligations to dedicate him- or herself to the quest for liberation (*mokṣa*). Such persons no longer see themselves as a part of the fabric of society. In the *Bhagavadgītā*, however, Kṛṣṇa tells us who is the true renunciant:

> One who performs one's duty without seeking its personal fruit is the *sannyāsin*, the yogi; not one who is without the sacred fire and who performs no actions (6:1).

The heart of renunciation is not inactivity, but the performance of unselfish action. In other words, mere abstinence from the kinds of activity in which the person with a family (*gṛhastya*) may engage for the care and support of that family does not make one a renunciant. The term *niragnir* (without sacred fire) refers to the fact that becoming a *sannyāsin* absolves one from the necessity to perform daily rituals consisting of offerings through the sacred fire. Neither the renunciation of obligatory actions in society nor the giving up of traditional forms of worship makes one a *sannyāsin* (renunciant).

Throughout the *Bhagavadgītā*, Kṛṣṇa emphasizes the inward attitude of renunciation. Since actions, as we have seen, can never be completely avoided, the renunciant is one who can be active in the world without desire for personal rewards.

> It is indeed impossible for an embodied being to renounce actions entirely. But one who renounces the personal fruits of action is regarded as a renunciant (18:11).

Chapter 5

"One Who Hates No Being, Friendly and Compassionate" (12:13)

In chapter 4, we saw that through a correct understanding of the *ātman* one gains self-acceptance. Knowing the Self to be *ānanda* (fullness) enables one to perform actions from joy. This knowledge does not deprive the *jñānī* of all motivation for action, but inspires such a person to live and work for the happiness of others. The *jñānī* is twice described in the *Bhagavadgītā* (5:25; 12:4) as one who rejoices in the well-being of all (*sarvabhūtahite ratāḥ*).

Peace with oneself and joyful work in the service of others are vital qualities of the ideal person in the *Bhagavadgītā*. One who delights in working for the welfare of others is richly endowed with the virtues of love and compassion. It should not surprise us, therefore, to find Kṛṣṇa including these qualities in his characterization of the *jñānī* (wise person).

In chapter 12, Kṛṣṇa begins a detailed portrait of the qualites of the devotee (*bhakta*).

> *adveṣṭā sarvabūtānāṁ maitraḥ karuṇa eva ca*
> *nirmamo nirahaṁkāraḥ samaduḥkhasukhaḥ kṣamī*
>
> One who hates no being, who is friendly and compassionate, without possessiveness and egoism, balanced in pleasure and pain and forgiving (12:13).

This verse is particularly important in its structure. Kṛṣṇa begins with the statement that the devotee is free from hate. This condition could be interpreted as indicating neutrality or indifference towards others, for an indifferent person may also be free from hate. To affirm, however, that he is speaking about a warm and positive attitude, Kṛṣṇa follows his opening statement with the words *maitraḥ* (friendly) and *karuṇa* (compassionate). Friendship toward others and compassion for those who suffer are the opposite of indifference and lack of care.

Throughout the *Bhagavadgītā*, Kṛṣṇa reiterates and emphasizes the fact that proper understanding of the *ātman* results in relationships of compassion toward all beings. One of my favorite verses on this theme occurs in chapter 6:

> *ātmaupamyena sarvatra samaṁ paśyati yo 'rjuna*
> *sukhaṁ vā yadi vā duḥkhaṁ sa yogī paramo mataḥ*
>
> One who, through the sameness of the Self, sees with equality everywhere, in pleasure or in pain, is regarded as the best Yogī (6:32).

As human beings, we experience our bodies and minds and respond appropriately to their respective conditions. Pain in the body or worry in the mind elicits a response of concern and discomfort. It is natural to act compassionately toward oneself to be rid off such pain and worry.

An entirely selfish person (and it is questionable whether such a person exists) is someone capable of responding only to his or her own needs and who finds it impossible to reach out to others. Most of us can identify with and become involved in meeting the needs of others. We do this to different degrees and within different limits and boundaries.

For some of us, the circle of identity extends to our immediate or extended families and friends. We are moved by their joys and sorrows as if these were our own. Nothing outside of this circle touches us, and the pains of others beyond the circle are always distant and remote. For others, this circle may be expanded to include those who live in the same village or town or in the same country. It may even stretch across national boundries to include those belonging to the same religion or ethnic group. For most of us, though, the circles of our identity and compassion have clear limits, whether these limits are defined by family, nation, ethnic group, or religion.

Chapter 6:32 speaks of the ideal person as one who identifies with all and whose compassion knows no limits. The term *sarvatra* suggests both everyone and everywhere. It refers to the overcoming of geographical, national, linguistic, cultural, and ethnic barriers. In other words, the wider the circles of our identities, the better our lives reflect the truth of the *ātman*. Ultimately, limits and boundaries should fall and one should respond to the joys and sorrows (*sukhaṁ vā yadi vā duḥkhaṁ*) of beings everwhere.

It is important to note that Kṛṣṇa not only speaks of responding to the pain of others but to their joy as well. We should neither be envious of the happiness and success of others nor take delight in their pains and disappointments. These kinds of responses only enclose us more firmly within the narrow and painful confines of our egos, veiling from us that full Self which is the same in all beings.

The famous Hindu teacher Rāmānuja provides one of the finest examples of compassion. According to tradition, Rāmānuja goes to his teacher and asks to be initiated into the spiritual life. The teacher gives him the sacred name of God and instructs him never to disclose the name to anyone else. The punishment for revealing the name to another, warns the teacher, is life in hell. Rāmānuja immediately goes to the top of the local temple and shouts, "I am going to give you all a name which will save you. My teacher has given me the sacred name of God." He shouts the name loudly for all to hear. The teacher hears of Rāmānuja's actions and summons him to inquire about the violation of his instruction. Rāmānuja's answer is simple and direct: "I am prepared to go to hell a hundred times, if I can save thousands."[1]

Chapter 6 of the *Bhagavadgītā* not only offers us an ideal, but also gives a method for the realization of unqualified love. This method is suggested in the term *ātmaupamyena*, a compound of *ātma* (Self) and *aupamyena* (sameness). Kṛṣṇa's teaching here is that, like ourselves, all beings have the same needs for avoiding pain and attaining happiness. Even as we do not intentionally inflict pain on ourselves, we should not cause pain to others. We cannot wish for a life of happiness for ourselves while denying the same to others. We cannot struggle for our own freedom, justice, and dignity while being unjust and contemptuous to others. We cannot expect to be loved by others if we do not share love. We must therefore enter with compassion into the lives of others, learning to see through their eyes, share their feelings, understand their thoughts, and respond to their needs. The one who can do this, says Kṛṣṇa, is the supreme Yogī. The *Bhagavadgītā* ideal is not indifference and the severing of relationships, but love and compassion.

Why is it desirable to identify with others and to consider their joys and sorrows our own? The concept of *ātmaupamyena* (sameness of Self) provides a justification and answer. In this concept we have the most profound teaching of the *Bhagavadgītā* — that the *ātman* is identical in all beings. This is a truth Kṛṣṇa repeatedly affirms in the text. Chapter 13:27 contains a beautiful statement of it:

samaṁ sarveṣu bhūtesu tiṣṭhantaṁ parameśvaram
vinaśyatsv avinaśyantaṁ yaḥ paśyati sa paśyati

One who sees the Supreme Lord abiding equally in all beings, the imperishable in the perishable, truly sees.

For the discerning Hindu, God has the highest value and is the focus of deepest love and loyalty. God is the true end of all seeking, the destiny of life's journey. God is the eternal truth which we long for amidst all that is fleeting and transient, the lasting joy amidst transient pleasures.

It is God's existence in all beings that gives them value and significance. The *Bhagavadgītā* calls us to rejoice in the well-being of others because that which we hold to be ultimately valuable dwells within them. Every being is sacred and worthy of reverence on account of the reality of God within.

An important implication of this central Hindu insight is that no created and, therefore, finite and perishable object ought ever to become the object of our worship and veneration *for its own sake*. This indeed would constitute idolatry, which is the false substitution of the finite for the infinite, the noneternal for the eternal. In the profuse use of *mūrtis* (icons) to represent God in worship, the Hindu must be vigilant that the image does not become an end in itself, a substitute for God who, while indwelling all things, transcends the limits of all forms.

The Hindu teaching about God's existence in all beings is always carefully explained in the *Bhagavadgītā* by two significant disclosures, both of which are logical and consistent with the nature of God. The first disclosure is that God is present in all beings (*sarveṣu bhūteṣu tiṣṭhantaṁ parameśvaram*). With regard to the presence of God, therefore, all beings must be equally regarded. No one is excluded and there are no qualifications which can be introduced here.[2] This is an essential truth which must be vigorously defended. It cannot be argued that God dwells in men and and not in women, in select ethnic groups or among the followers of particular religions. Similarly, the assignment of human beings to different castes and the varying value placed upon them with respect to caste is clearly called into question by this basic Hindu teaching. We must be prepared to question and challenge any authority — human or textual — which sanctions the unjust and oppressive treatment of others.

To avoid the widow by regarding her as inauspicious, to reject the birth of a girl by considering her less desirable than a boy, to mistreat the elderly and discriminate against the disabled are all expressions of blindness to God's indwelling presence. The Sanskrit term *bhūta* is inclusive, incorporating all beings. The presence of God is not limited to the human species, so we must also discern God in other-than-human life-forms. These forms must be within the reach of our concern and compassion. Our understanding of God grows as we learn to recognize God's presence in them.

The second disclosure about God's presence lies in the emphasis on the equality (*samaṁ*) of that presence. God's reality is not greater or lesser in any being. Our knowledge of God's presence may differ and so may the extent to which it influences our attitudes and ways of living. Human beings are unique in having the ability to know God and to express this knowledge in relationships of love and compassion. There is no question, however, of different degrees of God's presence in beings. Kṛṣṇa sees it necessary to emphasize the *equality* of God's presence along with its *inclusiveness*, since an argument that the degree of God's presence varies from being to being may be used to justify preferential regard for some and injustice toward others.

To profess love and loyalty for God while acting inconsiderately to others is a clear indication of spiritual ignorance and blindness. We truly begin to see and our understanding blossoms when the love which fills our hearts for God in worship reaches out to touch every being and infuses each act with compassion. Every human encounter becomes joyful, for in each one we behold our Beloved. There is no human being so fallen or depraved in whom one cannot see the indwelling of God. To miss the equality of God's presence is self-destructive.

> Because one who sees the Lord seated the same everywhere destroys not the Self by the Self and attains, therefore, the highest goal (13:28).

To see God in all beings is not an act of physical perception through which we detect a new form. Here, seeing involves learning to look at all things with a new understanding and wisdom. The ordinary becomes extra-ordinary by being viewed as the abode of the eternal.

Notes

1. Adapted from Swami Ramdas, *Stories as Told by Swami Ramdas*, p. 51.

2. See also *Bhagavadgītā*, 10:20 and 18:61.

Chapter 6

"Sense-Pleasures Have a Beginning and an End" (5:22)

The *Bhagavadgītā*, as we have seen, offers us a knowledge which enables us to be at peace with ourselves, to perform actions with joy, and to lead lives of love and compassion. Another important and relevant value which follows from the knowledge of the *ātman* and which is vital to the Hindu way of life is self-control (*ātmavaśaḥ*). Throughout the *Bhagavadgītā*, Kṛṣṇa emphasizes self-control, presenting it as a vital expression of wisdom and as a necessary value in the life of anyone who aspires to Self-knowledge.

The exercise and practice of self-control is unique to us as human beings. As a species, we enjoy a certain freedom of choice which allows us to act in ways that are not always conducive to our own well-being or to the happiness of others. The behavior of other-than-human life-forms, in contrast, is governed and regulated by instinct, with little room for freedom of choice. When we fail to exercise self-control, we give up a characteristic distinctive to us, losing a unique quality of our humanity.

In so many ways our life-styles today reflect the absence of self-control. We become slaves to every physical urge and mental fancy, unintelligently pursuing every new craze and fad. In refusing to exercise our precious gift of freedom, we allow ourselves to become mindlessly obedient to the will of others.

This self-destructive abandonment of freedom is certainly not the ideal which the *Bhagavadgītā* holds before us. As we saw earlier, at the end of chapter 2 Arjuna asks Kṛṣṇa to describe the person whose understanding of the Self is stable. After first mentioning that such a person is internally at peace, Kṛṣṇa immediately turns to the quality of self-control and uses a beautiful example to explain the control which Self-knowledge brings.

> When like a tortoise, which withdraws its limbs from all sides, one can withdraw the senses from the sense objects, then one's understanding is firm (2:58).

Whenever it senses the smallest hint of danger, the tortoise withdraws its limbs into its shell as a form of protection. It extends and retracts its limbs at will, demonstrating its firm control over its body. Similarly, says Kṛṣṇa, the person of mature wisdom can withdraw the senses from the sense-objects when indulgence becomes harmful to the self and painful to others. The point of the example is to show that the senses of the *jñānī* are under the *jñāni*'s control and freedom of choice has not been lost.

Why is self-control such an important mark of wisdom? And how can we strive to attain it? Self-control requires a twofold adjustment in our lives. We need to cultivate a new relationship with the objects of the world as well as with other human beings.

What is the desirable relationship with the objects of the world? For an answer, let us look at the following passage from the *Bhagavadgītā*:

> *ye hi saṁsparśajā bhogā duḥkhayonaya eva te*
> *ādyantavantaḥ kaunteya na teṣu ramate budhaḥ*
>
> The pleasures that are born out of contact between the senses and sense-objects are sources of unhappiness, Arjuna, since they have a beginning and an end; a wise person does not indulge in these (5:22).

The pleasures which we gain through the experience of sense-objects are momentary and fleeting; they leave us with a sense of want and dissatisfaction. This drives us to seek again the same object or another. Before long, we are helplessly addicted, dependent, and unhappy.

The pleasure of a sense-object is never lasting because the factors involved are unstable and continuously changing. The object diminishes and is reduced with enjoyment, the sense-organ ages and is worn with excessive enjoyment, and the mind grows tired and satiated with repeated indulgence and yearns for new pleasures. We find ourselves in a vicious circle. We seek a lasting fullness, but we search for this through impermanent objects and experiences. These leave us dissatisfied, so we turn again to the same transient objects and experiences. To appreciate that the lasting joy and peace we seek cannot be found in the temporary pleasures of the senses is an important mark of wisdom necessary for self-control.

One of the finest examples of this wisdom occurs in the parable of the *Kaṭha Upaniṣad*. In this *Upaniṣad* we are introduced to Vajasravas, the father of Naciketa. Vajasravas is performing the *Viśvajit Yajña*, a sacrifice in which one is expected to distribute one's possessions. Naciketa, however, observes that his father is giving away only those cows which are barren and not expected to live long. Observing this serious defect in the performance of the ritual, Naciketa becomes concerned for his father's welfare. He knows his father will not attain the heavenly world by being so miserly. Naciketa thinks that by offering himself, he can correct the defect in his father's charity.

Approaching his father, he repeatedly asks, "Father, to whom will you offer me?"[1] Exploding with anger, Vajasravas declares, "To Death, I offer you." Naciketa reaches the abode of Yama, the god of death, and patiently awaits the return of Yama, who is not home. Troubled that Naciketa has waited on him for three nights without the customary hospitality afforded, Yama offers him three boons of his choice.

For his first boon, Naciketa requests that his father be cheerful and free from anger towards him. For his second, he requests the knowledge of a ritual which leads to the gain of heaven (*svarga loka*). Urged by Yama to claim his third boon, Naciketa asks a question: "When a person dies, there is this doubt: some say he exists, some again say he does not. This I should like to know, being taught by you. This is the third of my boons."

Yama, however, is not immediately ready to explain the mystery of life and death to Naciketa, so he offers him various enticements as alternatives to spiritual instruction. "Choose sons and grandsons," says Yama, "who will live a hundred years, herds of cattle, elephants, horses and gold; choose a vast territory on earth, and live yourself as many years as you desire. . .. Whatever objects of desire are difficult to get in this world of mortals do you ask for them all according to your choice. . .. But Naciketa do not ask about death."

Naciketa responds with an answer full of wisdom about the

limitations of sense-pleasures.

> All these are transient and they wear out the vigor of the senses. All life, without exception, is short. Keep your horses, dances, and songs for yourself.[2]

Naciketa realizes that even though Yama could increase the length of his life, its span would be still finite. The many objects of pleasure would only provide him with limited enjoyment, and indulgence would wear him down physically. The most important statement in his reply to Yama occurs, however, in I.i.27: "A human being," affirms Naciketa, "will never find fullness in wealth."[3] In other words, there is no hope of reaching a point of contentment through the multiplication of one's material possessions or life-span. Such a search is without any end or destination, a race without a finishing line.

Why do we feel this unquenchable thirst for objects even beyond the point when our basic needs are satisfactorily met? A principal reason must be the false value and emphasis which we give to these objects. We can never have enough when our material possessions are acquired to fulfill psychological rather than physical needs. Let us take the simple example of clothing. The original purpose for wearing clothes must be connected with the need to protect ourselves from the harshness of climate and environment and to preserve our modesty. These needs still exist, but they cannot explain the variety and quantity of clothing we may possess. For many of us, clothing is part of our effort to be acceptable to ourselves and to others. How many suits of clothing does one need to satisfy this psychological need? Obviously, there is no limit.

What is true of clothing is also true of many other objects in our lives. Appreciating that material objects will always leave us wanting is a necessary step in developing self-control and having a mature, intelligent relationship with objects in the world.

It is necessary to emphasize, however, that Hinduism does not equate wealth with evil. Hinduism is not an antimaterialistic tradition. The necessity and significance of wealth is recognized in the fact that *artha* (wealth) is one of the four legitimate ends of human existence along with *kāma* (pleasure), *dharma* (virtue) and *mokṣa* (liberation).[4] But when the concern for wealth so dominates our lives that our understanding of who we are and our sense of self-worth are identified with our possessions, then we have lost control and allowed wealth to dominate our lives. Wealth also controls our lives when we judge and value the worth of other human beings on the basis of their material assets.

We have discussed the need and justification for self-control in relation to sense-objects and our material wants. The human sexual urge, however, is as powerful as the drive for material things and also requires the exercise of restraint. There is a critical need for self-control in the arena of human sexuality.

Critics have often dismissed Hinduism as otherworldly and life-denying, and this has led many to expect the attitude of the Hindu tradition to be one of rejection and revulsion to all forms of sense-enjoyment. This is certainly not true. *Kāma* (pleasure) is recognized as a legitimate human pursuit. Hinduism has not taken sense-enjoyment to be life's highest end, but neither has it condemned sense-enjoyment as evil. In the *Bhagavadgītā*, Kṛṣṇa teaches that he is the principle of pleasure which is not opposed to morality (*dharmāviruddho bhūteṣu kāmo 'smi bharatarṣabha*) (7:11).

Like all other natural urges, the sexual impulse can be both legitimately used as well as abused. From a Hindu standpoint, it is abused when allowed to so dominate us that we lose sight of life's higher purposes. Hinduism stands opposed to any value system which makes the gratification of bodily impulses its highest end. The preservation of this Hindu position may indeed be one of the most difficult challenges we face in contemporary society, where we are bombarded with sexual images.

There is a clear recognition of the legitimacy of sexuality in human existence, but to treat and view the human body simply as an instrument of pleasure is to miss its unique nature as an instrument for the gain of Self-knowledge and liberation. It is, in the words of Tulasidasa in the *Uttarakāṇḍa* of the *Rāmacaritamānasa*, a location for spiritual discipline (*sādhana dhāma*) and a doorway to liberation (*mokṣakara dvāra*).

Similarly, to look upon others solely as objects of one's sexual enjoyment is to miss the presence of the sacred in each one. One who allows the sexual urge to exercise control over one's life has lost his or her freedom and is on a certain road to frustration and unhappiness.

The proper place of sexuality, in the Hindu view, is in the committed life of a loyal and happy marriage. Such loving relationships are seen as vital for one's spiritual growth. We know also, today, that they are the best guarantee of one's physical health and well-being.

Notes

1. *pitaram tata kasmai mām dāsyasīti*
(*Kaṭha Upaniṣad* I.i.4).

2. *śvobhāvā martyasya yadantakaitat*
sarvendriyāṇāṁ jarayanti tejaḥ
api sarvaṁ jīvitamalpameva
tavaiva vāhāstava nṛtyagīte
(*Kaṭha Upaniṣad* I.i.26).

3. *na vittena tarpaṇīyo manuṣyo* (*Kaṭha Upaniṣad* I.i.27).

4. For a discussion of the goals of Hindu life, see A. Rambachan, *The Hindu Vision*, Ch. 2.

Chapter 7

"Craving Vanishes When the Supreme Is Known" (2:59)

Self-control, as we have seen in chapter 6, is an important expression of Self-knowledge: "Knowledge is steady," says Kṛṣṇa, "only in the person whose senses are under control" (2:61).

Kṛṣṇa cautions us, however, that the power of the sense organs ought never to be underestimated. A single moment of inattentiveness may be enough to sweep one off the desired path.

> *yatato hy api kaunteya puruṣasya vipaścitaḥ*
> *indriyāṇi pramāthīni haranti prasabhaṁ manaḥ*
>
> The turbulent senses, even of a wise person who is practicing self-control, may forcibly carry away the mind (2:60).

The point here is that one can never become complacent about the need for self-control. The key terms in the above verse are *yatataḥ* (of the striving) and *vipaścitaḥ* (of the wise). The wise person is one who understands the limitations of the sense-objects and endeavors to attain control over the sense-organs. The mind, however, continues to be drawn to objects on the basis of long-established habits. Control can only be won by unbroken vigilance. The mind's tendency to flow in a particular direction does not disappear the moment one appreciates the limitations of such pursuits. Control is gained only through constant practice and repeated reflection on the limitations of sense-objects.

Arjuna himself, in the *Bhagavadgītā*, raises the important question of the control of the mind and senses.

> This Yoga of peacefulness which you describe is difficult to attain. How can the mind which is so restless attain peace?
>
> The mind, Kṛṣṇa, is indeed restless, stormy, strong, and stubborn. It is as difficult to restrain as the wind (6:33–34).

In his reply, Kṛṣṇa gives two successful techniques for achieving self- control.

> *asaṁśayaṁ mahābāho mano durnigrahaṁ calam*
> *abhyāsena tu kaunteya vairāgyeṇa ca gṛhyate*
>
> It is true, Arjuna, that the mind is restless and difficult to control. But it can be restrained by regular practice and detachment (6:36).

Although conceding that the challenge is a difficult one, Kṛṣṇa recommends *abhyaāsa* and *vairāgya*. *Abhyaāsa* is the constant practice of trying to steer the mind into new ways of thinking.

Even as old habits are formed by repeatedly thinking and acting in particular ways, so new habits must be cultivated by new patterns of thinking and acting. Each time one's thoughts flow in ways contrary to one's wisdom, the mind must be gently restrained and redirected. This process of retraining the mind is facilitated by *vairāgya*, the detachment that arises from repeatedly presenting to the mind the limitations of unrestrained sense-indulgence.

Self-control, it must be remembered, has nothing to do with starving oneself, denying the necessities of life, or tormenting the mind. Such practices will not help in attaining mental control. The *Bhagavadgītā* wisely recommends moderation in all activities:

> Yoga is not for one who eats too much or abstains too much from eating; it is not for one, Arjuna, who sleeps too much or keeps awake too much (6:16).

As Hastāmalaka, a disciple of Śaṅkara, reminds us in the *Bhaja Govindam*, even reducing one's necessities to the barest minimum does not bring about freedom from the grip of desires. He gives us a graphic picture of pseudo-asceticism.

> In front, there is fire; at the back, there is the sun; in the night, (the ascetic sits) with the knees stuck to the chin; he receives alms in his palms, and lives under trees; yet the bondage of desire does not leave him.[1]

The restlessness of the mind is an expression of its search for joy. It flits from object to object in the hope of finding a permanent source of satisfaction, even as a bee hums about anxiously from flower to flower in search of nectar. One must clearly appreciate that the agitations of the mind are expressions of its thirst for fullness. To seek to quell these agitations without resolving this basic need is impossible and frustrating. The meaningful method, as prescribed by Kṛṣṇa, is to understand the causes of the mind's restlessness, the limitations of sense pursuits, and the nature of the *ātman* as happiness.

Knowing the *ātman* as happiness is the lasting way to self-control. Once the mind has tasted the joy of the Self, it will naturally turn to that source again and again, growing detached from the limited pleasures of sense attractions. A prisoner, for example, may be unable to participate in certain forms of enjoyment available to free people. The longing for these enjoyments, however, continues to grow in the prisoner's mind, and the prisoner will seek fulfillment when freedom is gained. Similarly, even though one may forcibly restrain the senses from their respective objects, one's craving for these objects continues to grow in the mind. Such craving, says Kṛṣṇa, vanishes when the fullness of the *ātman* is known.

> Though aspirants abstain from sense-pleasures, they will still crave for them. Even this craving, however, vanishes when the Supreme is known (2:59).

The ideal of Hinduism is not withdrawal from or fear of life. It does not require that we condemn the world as an undesirable place of evil. It seeks, instead, to help us to develop a healthy and mature relationship with the world. An important aspect of this mature relationship requires that we know the limitations of the objects in the world to satisfy our desire for happiness. This knowledge seeks to protect us from the disappointments of making sense enjoyment the sole end of our lives. The Hindu ideal is beautifully summed up by Kṛṣṇa.

> The person excels, Arjuna, who, restraining the senses by the mind, unattached, directs his energies to the path of work (3:7).

Knowledge of the Self, as we have seen, helps us to correct our relationship with the world of objects. This wisdom also helps us develop healthy relationships with other human beings. These relationships are among our most valued and precious assets as we travel the journey of life. They can be helpful in promoting our spiritual growth, but they can also be stumbling blocks that make our journeys slow and painful. Let us look at examples of both kinds of relationships.

According to a traditional account, Tulasīdāsa, the author of the popular *Rāmacaritamānasa*, was deeply attached to his wife Devi Mamata.[2] It is said that he could never endure separation from her. One day, King Akbar was going on a tour and Tulasīdāsa joined the king's party. Soon after his departure, a messenger arrived from the home of his wife's parents, informing her that her mother was ill and requesting her to come at once. Devi Mamata obtained permission to go from her mother-in-law and left for her parents' home.

When Tulasīdāsa returned home late that evening and was told of his wife's departure, he could not rest. He immediately walked the ten miles to the home of his father-in-law. It was late at night and the doors were locked. He saw what he thought what was a rope hanging from the balcony of his wife's room, caught it, and climbed into the house.

Devi Mamata was astonished to see her husband. "Why did you leave me and come here?" inquired Tulasīdāsa, "I had to walk ten miles in order to find you." Devi Mamata was enraged: "How did you enter the house?" she asked. "I used the rope which you kindly left hanging from the balcony," answered Tulasīdāsa. "Why do you tell such lies?" retorted his wife, "I never left a rope there for you. Show it to me." With the help of a servant, a huge poisonous snake was found hanging from the balcony.

"You think of yourself as wise and clever," argued Devi Mamata, "but you are full of ignorance. Why did you leave the safety of your home, risking your life, to come here at this late hour? If a tiny portion of your attachment to me was directed to the feet of God, how easily you would find Him!"

Mamata's statement was a eye-opener for Tulasīdāsa and a turning point in his life. His relationship with her was one not of love but of infatuation and attachment. He was extremely possessive of her and completely dependent. While it is true that persons who love each other enjoy each other's company and are happy to be together, this love must be distinguished from possessiveness. Tulasīdāsa's obsession with Mamata was a source of pain for her and a cause of unhappiness to both of them.

In the *Bṛhadāraṇyaka Upaniṣad*, we have the example of a contrasting relationship, one between Yājñavalkya and Maitreyī. Yājñavalkya informs Maitreyī of his decision to enter the stage of renunciation (*saṅnyāsa*) and to distribute his wealth between his two wives, Maitreyī and Kātyāyanī. Maitreyī immediately asks whether she would gain immortality through wealth. Yājñavalkya explains that her life would be similar to the lives of those who possess in abundance, but immortality could not be attained through wealth (*amṛtatvasya tu nāśāsti vitteneti*). "What shall I do with that which will not make me immortal?" asks Maitreyī. "Tell me of that alone, which you know (to be the only means of immortality)."

Using examples of different relationships, Yājñavalkya explains to Maitreyī the true object of love.

> It is not for the sake of the husband, my dear, that he is loved, but for the sake of the *ātman* that he is loved. It is not for the sake of the wife, my dear, that she is loved, but for the sake of the *ātman* that she is loved.[3]

Yājñavalkya's point is insightful. In the love of another, the real object of attraction is neither the physical body nor the mind. The body, after all, is only lifeless matter. It gains its life, luster, and ability to function only because of the presence of the Self. The skin has the capacity to feel, the eyes to see, the ears to hear, the nostrils to smell, and the tongue to taste only because the light that is the Self shines in the senses. The *Kena Upaniṣad* beautifully describes the dependence of the senses on the *ātman*.

> That which the eyes cannot see, but by which the eyes see, know that alone to be *brahman*, not that which is worshipped here (as an object).
>
> That which the ear cannot hear, but by which the ear is able to hear, know that alone to be brahman, not that which is worshipped here (I:7–8).

What is true of the body is also true of the mind. Like the body, the mind cannot generate thoughts and emotions without the light of awareness that is the *ātman*. How can there be any thoughts without awareness? As the teacher in the *Kena Upaniṣad* again reminds us,

> That which the mind cannot think of (as an object), but by which the mind thinks, know that alone to be *brahman*, not that which is worshipped here (I:6).

The life and luminosity of the body and mind are borrowed. The true object of love and attraction is the immortal, blissful *ātman*. Even as a fire can transmit its heat to a cold piece of iron and make it glow, so does the *ātman* lend its beauty to the body and mind. A lifeless body, Śaṅkara reminds us in the *Bhaja Govindam*, ceases to have any attraction.

> As long as there is breath in the body, so long do people in the household ask about one's welfare. Once the breath leaves, on the destruction of the body, the dependents dread that very same body.[4]

When we understand that the true object of love in each one is the *ātman*, our love gains depth and permanence. It becomes free from selfishness and attachment. We can appreciate the beauty of the physical body and the brilliant wonders of the human mind, seeing their origin and dependence in the limitless Self. Tulasıdāsa had little regard for the well-being of Mamata. It was his need that mattered above all else. Love is selfless and, when its basis is in the immortal *ātman*, it is indeed eternal. This is the love to which Kṛṣṇa calls us in the *Bhagavadgītā* and which his teaching makes possible.

Notes

1. *agre vahniḥ pṛṣthe bhānū*
   rātrau cubukasamarpitajānuḥ
   karatalabhikṣas tarutalavāsa-
   stadapi na muñcaty -āśāpāśaḥ
   (*Bhaja Govindam, 16*).

2. See J. E. Abbott and N. R. Godbole, *Stories of Indian Saints*, pp. 31–56.

3. *na vā are patyuḥ kāmāya patiḥ priyo*
   bhavati/ ātmanastu kāmāya patiḥ priyo
   bhavati/ na vā are jāyāyai kāmāya jāyā
   priyā bhavati/ ātmanastu kāmāya jāyā priyā
   bhavati (*Bṛhadāraṇyaka Upaniṣad,* II.4.5).

4. *yāvat pavano nivasati dehe*
   tāvat pṛcchati kuśalaṁ gehe

gatavati vāyau dehāpāye
bhāryā bibhyati tasmin kāye
(*Bhaja Govindam, 6*).

Works Cited

Abbot, J. E. and Godbole, N. R. *Stories of Indian Saints.* Delhi: Motilal Banarsidass, 1982.

Bhagavadgītā. Trans., S. Radhakrishnan. London: Allen and Unwin, 1956.

Bhagavadgītā: with Commentary by Swami Chinmayananda. Bombay: Central Chinmaya Mission Trust, n.d.

Bṛhadāraṇyaka Upaniṣad: with the Commentary of Śaṅkarācārya. Trans., Swami Madhavananda. Calcutta: Advaita Ashrama, 1975.

Kaṭhopaniṣad. Trans., Swami Sarvananda. Madras: Sri Ramakrishna Math, 1968.

Kenopaniṣad. Trans., Swami Sarvananda. Madras: Sri Ramakrishna Math, 1970.

Mahadevan, T. M. P., trans. *The Hymns of Śaṅkara.* Delhi: Motilal Banarsidass, 1980.

Rambachan, Anantanand. *The Hindu Vision.* Delhi: Motilal Banarsidass, 1992.

____. *Hanumān: The Messenger of God.* Minnesota: Vijnana Publications, 1990.

Sri Ramakrishna Math. *Tales and Parables of Sri Ramakrishna.* Madras: Sri Ramakrishna Math, 1980.

Swami Ramdas. *Stories as Told by Swami Ramdas.* Bombay: Bharatiya Vidya Bhavan, 1969.

Index